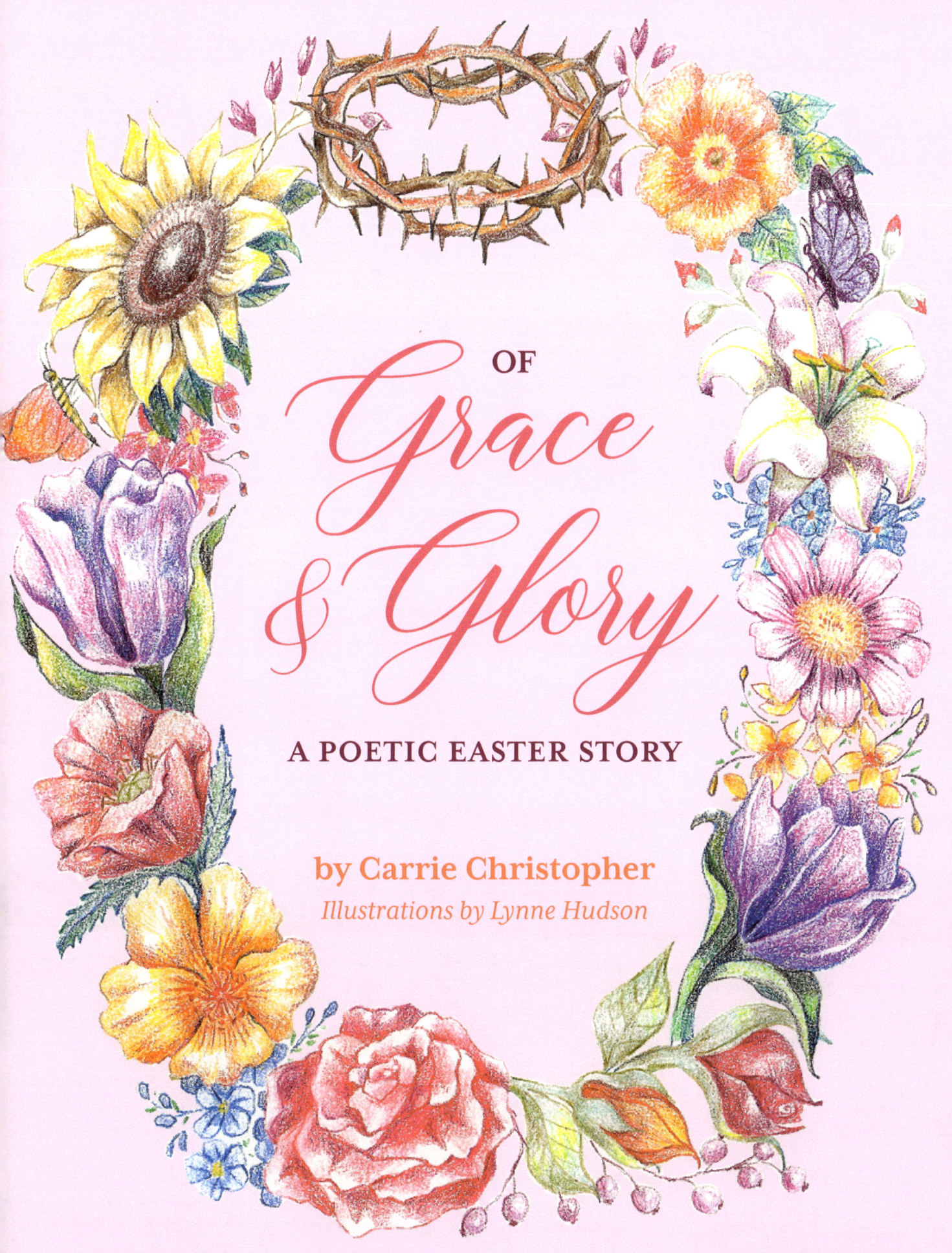

THIS BOOK IS LOVINGLY DISTRIBUTED BY:

Lionheart Ministry

Roaring with His ferocious love, calling the church to repentance, restoration, and revival.

Explore the ministry by visiting | www.lionheartministry.com

For God so loved the world that he gave his one and only Son, *that whoever* believes *in him* shall not perish but have *eternal* life.

For God did not send his Son into the world to condemn the world, but to *save* the world through *him*. *Whoever believes in him* is not condemned, but whoever does not believe stands *condemned* already because they *have not* believed *in the name* of God's one and *only* Son.

John 3:16-18 NIV

Deep, deep, deep within the ever-flowing streams of mercy, there laid a promise, written inside the depths of our Father's heart. This promise, the one true answer to the Fall, was nestled, lavished, held securely and intended for a song of deliverance to be the cure for humanity's aches.

His people were wailing, not prevailing, wasting away beneath the riddles of sin, struck down by the curses of humanity.

There they were screaming, inwardly and outwardly. Lingering on was a generation of lost souls, yearning and groaning for a Savior. A Savior to save His people from their sins.

This was the day that all had been waiting for, a hope to be secured. The only way to save a people from their sins was through the rugged way of the cross.

A cross full of redeeming love, beholding our very own Jesus, who was born roughly 33 years before, now sent to save the world from their sins.

How could it be that the King of all Kings would dare to taste sin's death on behalf of a guilty generation? That He should pardon to us a verdict of grace in spite of our rebellious sin crimes?

Oh, if we could see the full picture from Heaven, as His eyes roamed the earth. Glaring were the hardened hearts of men, as boisterous pride and selfish roots had been growing in and through His people for so so long!

This was the ultimate redemption plan, positioned and ready to be released. Goodness and mercy prevailed when the Father kissed His son goodbye and sent Him into humanity, in the flesh, down to earth on our behalf.

Prevailing intercessory tears majestically fell from Jesus' humble face, pouring out groaning grace. There on the cross, streaming from Jesus' eyes was the epitome of love.

Oh the blood that dripped, carelessly caused by others' hardened hearts, the rejection of truth, now flushed into the earth by way of suffering on the cross. This was the very earth that He created as His own. Now His blood was watering His garden. Once a garden of perfection created by His very hands, now the red tear-stained soil gathered at the foot of the cross, representing a grace garden of mercy.

His agony cried out in love during a death like no other. His voice bellowed, quaked and ached the world away in an awesome display of heroic intervention. He came for us. The one and only triune God, Jesus, Himself. Embodied with the Word, carrying a ferocious love.

He nailed every guilty, rebellious, sin of ours to the cross of death. Nailing it once and for all. With a humble intent to undo what occurred during the Fall. You see, the Fall represented a saddened separation from the heart of our very own Father God. There was no other way of hope for humanity!

From the outside the plan looked and felt obsolete. How does a reigning sinless King of Israel perish?

And what purpose did this cross-filled agony accomplish? It seemed to everyone looking at His death that the greatest form of misery and injustice had occurred right before their very eyes.

There was Mary tucked in between a group of women witnessing the greatest atrocity, yet kissed with the most powerful promise of redemption. Humble travailing Mother Mary, now watching her own son perish, after He walked the earth with the explosive power of the Kingdom of God. Now He suffered for humanity's cause and was unjustly murdered by a multitude of mockers. The hands and hearts that He fed, now persecuted Him to the point of death.

"For the joy set before Him He endured the cross, scorning its shame, and sat down at the right hand of the throne of God." Hebrews 12:2

And there she was, huddled in a group of loving women who were called to be witnesses to an unfair, unjust trial! Mother Mary who birthed a Savior, now faced the death of her very own perfect son, sent to die upon a cross, taking the place of careless mockers and persecutors.

Jesus' care streamed from the cross like banners of unrelenting love; He would not die before He commissioned one of His disciples to take in His very own mother — desiring to protect, provide and give her grace to keep living. Jesus honors His own mother before a multitude.

Let us ponder, Mary as a mother, imagining what she saw, her son on the cross. The weight of affliction may have silenced her life forever. She may have felt she was receiving a death sentence herself? Not even her own husband was there to comfort and console her — commentators suggest father Joseph died years prior to the cross. Let it be assumed, the only way Mary survived this, was through intimacy with Jesus Himself or Our father in heaven providing a word of reassuring love. She must have been told or deep trust taught her that Jesus must suffer first before Salvation so that the lost generation could be secured.

She must have surrendered every motherly desire to control and accepted the will of her King at any cost. Her ever-growing, flowing faith in the goodness of God must have carried her through the worst possible day of her life here on earth. Here humble Mary wasn't just chosen to bring into life the presence of Emmanuel God with us, the perfect risen Savior of the world, but also to witness the last dying breath of her son in the flesh. What agony, what an unjust atrocity.

But isn't it like God to portray what looks contrary to humanity's understanding, to save the world through this potential disaster?

Here these people had long awaited the Messiah of the world. And now hope had seemingly died on a cross, surrounded by robbers and true lords of evil. Our Lord the guilt-free, sinless, spotless lamb had been sacrificed.

Of grace and glory would be the divine answer, wrapped up in the crux of the cross.

"For the joy set before him he endured the cross, scorning its shame, and sat down at the right hand of the throne of God."

HEBREWS 12:2 NIV

Our Prayer for You

Praying dear reader, that as you listen to His love, music and lyrics from Lindsey Sullivan that the peace-filled presence of God would invade and heal every barren hungry place in your soul. His cross was enough to free you from the curse of sin and shame. Be free in His presence. Soak by listening to His love.

Listen to His love

LYRICS WRITTEN BY LINDSEY SULLIVAN

MY BELOVED

One hundred twenty four thousand three hundred and nine
That's the number of hairs on your head, I counted each one
When you rise in the morning and you take your first breath
It's my life in your lungs, my heartbeat in your chest

Do you see how I love you?
You were my own design
When you look at my face, can you feel my delight?

Oh how I delight in you
My beloved

If you want we can walk
Hand in hand to the mountaintop
All the treasures of my heart
They were yours from the start

Do you see how I love you?
You were my own design
When you look at my face can you feel my delight?

SCAN THE
QR CODE
TO LISTEN.

For three hours before Jesus' final words, light perished, the world trapped under utter darkness. The legions of evil thought they destroyed the imperishable light of life forever. Imagine a community upheaval as the sun resisted to shine for three whole long, pain-filled hours.

Darkness thought it had won, thinking it succeeded in killing the one who came for you and for me.

But God's unfolding plans and heavenly omnipotence see behind, into the present and beyond the future. His eyes span the very earth in wisdom, and He prepares the most unseen, precise, power-filled plan. He provided the earth with a plan, even when it looked, felt and tasted like the end.

Jesus chose to commit His spirit after three travailing hours in the dark.

Can you see it? Can you feel it? He endured darkness and death, faced the most battle-ready, heavy intercession of vetting the weight of every antagonizing pain and shame. Sins' existence without Jesus would've separated each of us and generations behind and beyond from the Father's love in totality and permanence.

After the tenacious warring hours of darkness, the crumbling ground shook, and the temple's curtains were torn into two! The palace-like place of worship, now destroyed as an earthquake struck in violence! Men and women as witnesses declared the truth! Death brought truth! They could now see, this was the TRUE God, the Savior of the world. The mockery, claims and injustice now deemed as a false accusation.

At the appointed time of Jesus' death, the dead bodies of the Saints arose to life. Yes, the dead Christ-followers AROSE! The dead that had once been buried, now impossibly arose from the earth. As the flesh of Jesus perished, the once-dead were resurrected. Previously dirt-filled graves now open as human bodies became alive again to roam the earth. What a shocking, bone-chilling event in all of history, to witness this. This was a prophetic undercurrent of scripture — the dead that arose that day projected Jesus' upcoming resurrection. If anyone dared with spiritual eyes to see the correlation, hope wouldn't have died.

The power that quaked the earth mimicked the Father's aching, travailing heart that His one and only Begotten Son had to suffer for the rest of His children. The broken heart of God stirred the dead to awake, notioning to the remaining bystanders and soldiers the truth. You see, they could not escape the truth of the cross. The cross represented Jesus as Lord and Savior, the one and only way to redemption, the one and only freedom and forgiveness of one's sins! The only God above all other Gods.

The darkened day of death had no sting, as God's plan of overflowing, abundant display of love streamed and flowered from His son's sacrifice. Truth was known that day to all His offenders.

Truth seemed to bellow through the wind and the waves shouting, "You shattered the Savior's life here on earth, He was your only hope. But grace has a way of unending mercy. Grace grabs our hearts when we run away and rebel. Grace cascades over our lives when we are calloused to hear. Grace engulfs and pursues us when all hope has been lost. Hope will return."

Father Grace is the author of Jesus' story and the dominion of humanity. He is an invitational Father that provides for everything we need, allowing the sin stains of the earth to be washed clean by the blood of His Son. God fought on our behalf against the demonic powers and principalities of death, and satan's domain, so that His people could rise with resurrection eyes and face any form of evil.

His redemptive purposes renew and revive our unbelief and wayward sin with the healing cure of His abundant, soul-soothing love.

You see, this story doesn't end here!

"It is for freedom that Christ has set us free. Stand firm, then, and do not let yourselves be burdened again by a yoke of slavery."

GALATIANS 5:1 (NIV)

Our Prayer for You

Dearest reader. Bask in a heavenly encounter with God. He has triumphed over the cross to set you free! Listen to His love through the music and lyrics by Lindsey Sullivan.

Listen to His love
LYRICS WRITTEN BY LINDSEY SULLIVAN

LOOK AT THE CROSS

Oh how I love you
Oh how I long
To make you my own now
Through my only son

Because my love is with you
You're never too lost
If ever you wander
Just look at the cross

This is my love song
For you my dear
Oh how I love you
Won't you come near?
Look what I've done now
My blood is poured out
If ever you wonder
Just look at the cross
If ever you wonder
Just look at the cross

SCAN THE QR CODE TO LISTEN.

It was three days later that He arose. He arose in a triumphant display of great awe-shaking glory! When Jesus came out of the grace-filled tomb, He neatly folded His face cloth!

John 20:7 (ESV) and the face cloth, which had been on Jesus' head, not lying with the linen cloths but folded up in a place by itself.

Let me repeat, He took time to fold His face cloth. What a symbolic way of mysterious love that was streaming from His face cloth and represented a purpose. He left a face cloth of grace, laid out neatly for us to see. An invitation to know Him, see Him and trust in His way of life and teachings as the most life-giving, transcending wisdom offered to us. Commentaries say that past Jewish tradition was to leave a napkin folded if you were coming back to the meal! Jesus hadn't left us permanently! His neatly folded face cloth prophetically shined in great glory.

Jesus was named as the WORD in biblical texts. He is found in the Word, which is the essence of His being! The Word being alive and active has never died! You see, it was kept hidden for ages to come in our life-breathing manual of the Bible. But it saddens our Savior when we look at the very Word of God as a rule book. As a means to be accepted in His sight. As a Pharisee-like way to build up our self-worth and pride. As a half-truth, "half believe what you want" written testimony. The Word is God. You see, encountering the Word is encountering God. When you experience the soul-satisfying Word of the Lord, and look to Jesus as a relational Savior, you will be fed a feast of living waters. Fruit will flow and fruit will grow within because you're no longer looking at a word that is void of power. Jesus is the Word. He came to die on the cross for you and for me, for the least of these — no matter what we have done.

Shame doesn't get the last say and guilt doesn't get the last gut jab. We can live in a freedom era of Christ-like faith, grace and truly have the way of the cross to encounter God.

Jesus is the manifestation of the gospel. But don't miss it. You may have been preached to about the gospel and believed in the good news, but never encountered our Father's love and our Jesus' voice, and the Holy Spirit's companionship. It's not enough to believe in your mind and never fully trust in your heart! There must be head, heart and surrender.

Surrender to your Savior this Easter and encounter HIM. The risen one, the final.

The one truth and the life. The alpha and the omega.

You see, He is the beginning and the end, and trusting in both lays you securely in the arms of your Father.

As we read the word, we experience our Savior. As we trust in His grace, we encounter His heart. As we surrender our control, we experience a flood.

As we submit to His leading, we become filled with great faith.

As we lose it all here on earth, we gain imperishable treasures gifted from His heart that surpass all fleshly gain.

"Now the Lord is the Spirit, and where the Spirit of the Lord is, there is freedom." (2 Corinthians 3:17)

The cross means freedom.

Of grace and glory

LIES HIS UNFOLDING STORY

Our King of Kings

CHOSE US TO WORSHIP AND SING

We sing of the way, the truth and the life

WE SILENCE THE VERY ENEMY AND EARTHLY STRIFE

It was He, who commissioned

ON THE CROSS HUMBLY POSITIONED

Grace and glory to unfold

GIVING US ACCESS TO BEHOLD

The very love of our God

ARMING OUR FEET WITH GOOD-NEWS SHOES SHOD

Surrender every bit of your soul

BE FILLED BY THE POWER OF THE SPIRIT IN FULL

Filled and lavished with great grace and glory

DO NOT DELAY TO GO AND TELL HIS PROMISING LOVE STORY

"My sheep listen to my voice; I know them, and they follow me. I give them eternal life, and they shall never perish; no one will snatch them out of my hand. My Father, who has given them to me, is greater than all; no one can snatch them out of my Father's hand. I and the Father are one." (John 10:27-30 NIV)

Listen to His love
LYRICS WRITTEN BY LINDSEY SULLIVAN

ALL OF MY DAYS

If I could just see You
If I could just see Your face

If I could just know You
If I could just know Your ways

If I could just hold You
Feel the touch of Your warm embrace

Because this is my purpose
God I want to spend all
of my days
With You
With You

If I could just see You
If I could just see Your face

If I could just know You
God I want to know all of Your ways

If I could just hold You
Feel the touch of Your
warm embrace

Because this is my purpose
God I want to spend all
of my days
With You
With You

All of my days, God
You hold every one
And I'll never go back
to who I was before
With You

SCAN THE
QR CODE
TO LISTEN.

GRIPPED BY GRACE AND
Saved Under It

A gesture of His goodness, a measure of His kindness, God sent Jesus to awaken us with faith!

Invitational expressive love is yours.

You see, the Gospel of great grace frees us. The truest, purest form of love is hidden in the ages and made known, manifesting before us, as we look in wonder upon the cross of Christ. So often we put perfection onto the people we love and ourselves thinking that we can be good and right if we just try hard enough. Freedom comes when awakened to the gut-wrenching realization that we truly are imperfect, love-hungry, sinful human beings. When we run from the reality of our sin we are trapped in an endless prison of self-satisfying pleasures. But when we confess our sins, the cross of his endless love heals us. Radically we can be made new, we can receive new life by a confession of the heart that we are like sheep without a shepherd who have gone astray. We desperately need a shepherd savior to guide us toward the path of righteous saving grace. We need Christ in us to be saved.

It once was told in the great Book of Life, by a jailor who cried out for salvation asking, "What must I do to be saved?"

He then brought them out and asked, "Sirs, what must I do to be saved?" They replied, "Believe in the Lord Jesus, and you will be saved — you and your household." Acts 16:30-31(NIV)

Would you walk to a path of freedom and healing with me today? As we feast upon truth, love and hope. As we truly reckon the sin and shame within us and as we let all fall at His feet we can and we will be saved under the powerful awakening of His blood.

Jesus answered, "I am the way and the truth and the life. No one comes to the Father except through me. John 14:6 (NIV)

OUR CRIES FOR SALVATION

I believe, and I trust that Christ died for me. I give You my life so I can be free. Freely You gave and generously You save! I give You my life, I surrender my soul, I ask for forgiveness and for salvation under Your lordship of grace. I receive rivers of Your love, giving me abounding joy and hope! The wells of salvation have made me glad! You have a divine plan and purpose for my life! Show me who You are and who You've made me to be! Let me tread on the heights of Your Holy mountain! Let me hear your voice!

A HEARTFELT THANKS TO....

My Husband - Thank you for making it possible to produce yet another book under Lionheart Ministry. Your continued support, generosity, and love cheer us on in the Heavenlies. You launch us all as arrows in the Spirit. You are truly a servant of His — humbly making a way for God's people to worship Him. I couldn't do this without you Jonathan, my very best friend.

My Children - You both are the grand spokesmen of our King's great love. I am in awe of God's encouragement through you both. Every kind word, every brilliant idea, and all that you are, is such a reflection of Jesus. Thank you my little loves for all of your love. The Lord's plans for you soar you HIGH into His heavenly calling on your lives. Furthermore, thank you Micah for specifically teaching us about the dead being resurrected after Jesus rose from the grave! All this credit in that writing section goes to you buddy!

Lynne Hudson - Praising the Lord that your array of magnificent artwork is displayed so powerfully here on earth as it is in HEAVEN. I imagine one day meandering through your art gallery in the courts of Heaven, cherishing every single moment working together here on earth. Lynne you are one of the most brilliant, humble, loving artists of God I've ever witnessed.

Kayla Follin - Dearest one, you continue to climb great mountains of artistic victories here on earth. You amaze me that your mind and heart can string together all of our book visions and heartfelt desires. You splash colors upon the pages with His love. Thank you sweet sister for your faithfulness!

Lindsey Sullivan - Your voice rises high like fragrant incense of praise unto our Lord. The strength of the Lord is carried to the nations through your beautiful valiant voice. I am amazed at the Holy Spirit's power in and through you as you creativity write, praise and pour out your heart to Him. Thank you for carrying my own heart into your songs to our Savior.

www.ingramcontent.com/pod-product-compliance
Lightning Source LLC
Chambersburg PA
CBHW042054050526
44107CB00109B/1139